ROOTED

The Root. The Rise. The Overflow.

Moses Peraza

Still Light Press

ISBN: 979-8-9987936-1-5

Published by Still Light Press

Website: stilllightpress.com

Email: info@stilllight.com

This work is a piece of creative expression and is not intended to replace professional advice, diagnosis, or treatment. The author disclaims any liability for adverse reactions or consequences resulting from the use of suggestions or practices contained herein.

Printed in the United States of America

First Edition, 2025

Still Light
PRESS

$25.00
ISBN 979-8-9926836-0-8
52500>
9 798992 683608

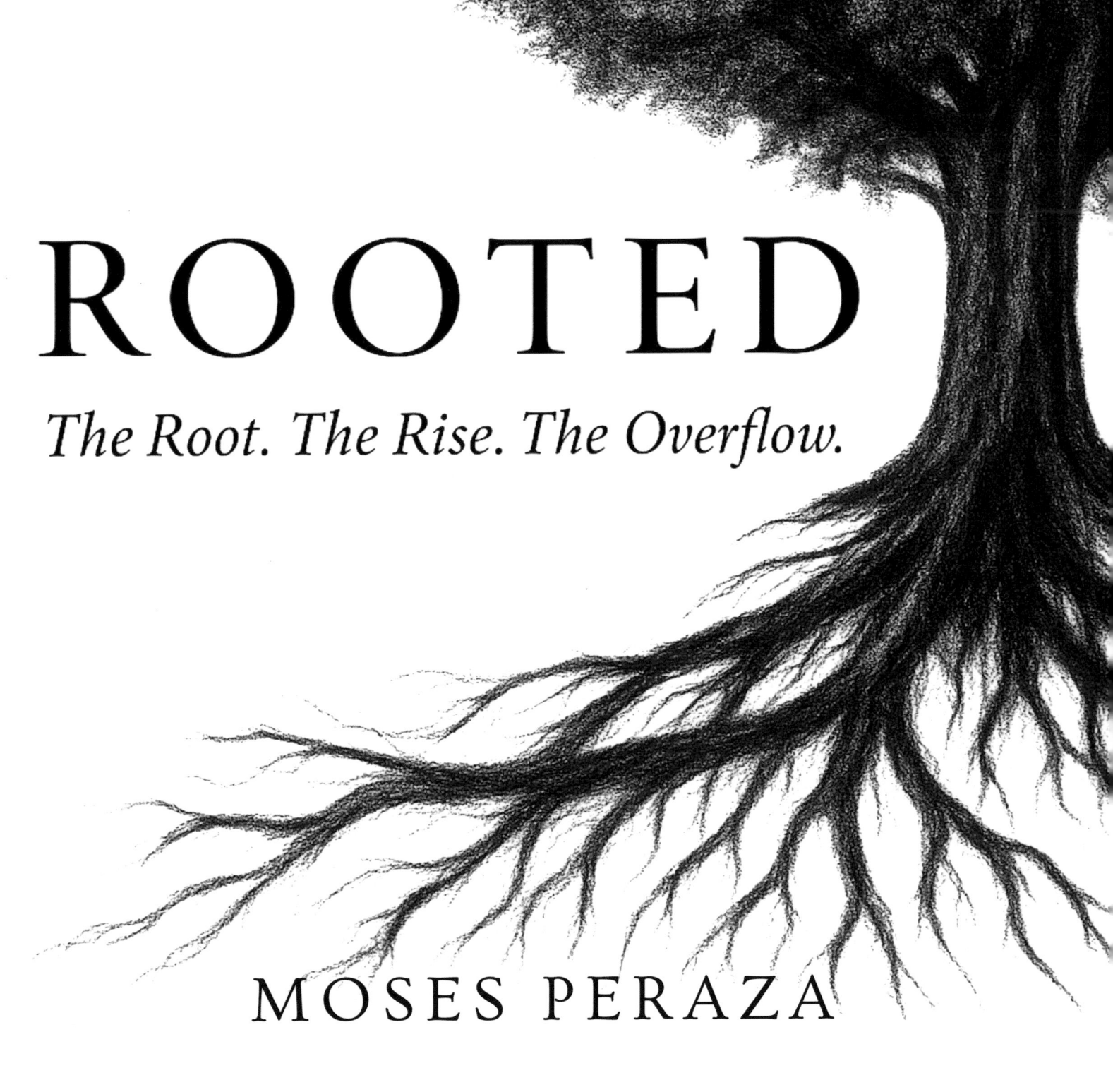

ROOTED

The Root. The Rise. The Overflow.

MOSES PERAZA

THIS BOOK
BELONGS TO

_____

the one who didn't call it growth,
just because it hurt.

the one who stayed
without applause,
beneath the surface,
beneath the noise.

You don't have to bloom to belong here.
You just have to keep coming back.

Before we rise, we must return.

Not to who we were,

but to the place beneath the noise.

This book is a remembering—

a call to sink into the soil of your soul,

to press your ear to the heartbeat

of your own life.

And to root.

Because what holds you, heals you.

Tending to Bloom

The seed was never the end
It was the silence that split —
the buried ache. The hidden yes.
And now?
The hand that planted it
repauses to kneel, to notice, to tend
Your roots do not need permission.
Your growth does not need applause.
This is not decoration.
This is becoming.
Your bloom is not fragile.
It is sacred.
It is already beginning.
Begin tending now.

YOU MUST STAY TO RISE

Not despite the silence.
But because of it.

THE FIRST
SPROUT

There was a sprout—
small, unsure,
pushing just barely above the skin of the soil.

It didn't rise in light.
It rose in aftermath.
In silence.
In a place where no one was watching.

It looked around and saw the tall things—
the trees already grown,
the flowers already blooming,
the wild ones who had always belonged.

And it thought:
I'm too late.
I'm too small.
I shouldn't be here.

The sprout almost curled back under.
The weight of being seen was too much.
The cold hadn't left its stem.

But then—
the soil whispered.

Not loud.
Not clear.
But just enough:

   "You are not fragile."
   "You are hidden."
   "You are becoming."

The wind came anyway.
The rain didn't hold back.
Nothing was spared.

But still—
the sprout stayed.
The sprout held.
The sprout reached.

Not because it felt strong,
but because something older than fear
told it to keep rising.

And that is what made it sacred.
Not the bloom.
Not the strength.
But the staying.

Even silence is becoming something.

You do not have to
bloom right away.

Rooted Through the Storms

You were not planted in peace.
You were planted in pressure.
And the storm did not wait for you to grow.

It came with winds.
With silence.
With tearing.

It stripped your leaves before they could unfurl.
It bent you in places no one could see.
It tried to make you forget the way down.

But still—
your roots remembered.

They held when your voice didn't.
They steadied what your heart hadn't caught up to.
They reached deeper every time the sky broke open.

This is what the storm taught you:
You are not breakable.
You are buried.
You are becoming.

What parts of you have stayed rooted—
even when you tried to leave them behind?

What did they know that you didn't?

You held.
And that was holy.

What happens when
you're seen before
you're ready?

BECOMING
SEEN

There was a stem
once quiet beneath the surface,
that had learned to grow by not being noticed.

It did not rise to be admired.
It did not stretch for the light.
It simply reached because it had to.

But then—
the wind shifted.
The earth gave way.
And light fell upon it.

And for the first time,
it was seen.

Not just touched by light,
but watched.
Named.
Noticed.

And it didn't know if this was
the miracle it had longed for—
or the beginning of something harder.

It had imagined that being seen
would feel like warmth.
Like sunlight soft across the skin.
Like being held without having to ask.

But it didn't expect the questions.
The comparisons.
The slow way some eyes admired
while others measured.

It didn't expect the weight
of being known.

There was no hiding now.
No soft place to go back to.
No soil to disappear into
without looking like retreat.

The light,
so soft at first,
now felt like a mirror
held too close.

And still—
the stem stayed.

It did not bloom.
It did not wither.

It just remained.

One day,
a soft rain came.
Not with thunder,
but with presence.

The light was still there.
But so was the stem.
Still standing.
Still real.
Still not blooming.

And something in the ground below whispered—

You do not need to open wide to be worthy.
You do not need to perform to belong.

You only need to remain.
To let yourself be seen
without shrinking.
Without hardening.
Without apologizing for what you are.

The stem did not rise any taller.
But it did not retreat.
And for that alone,
it became sacred.

You did not bloom.
You did not run.
You remained.
That was enough.

RETURNING
TO THE CENTER

When all the layers fell away,
When all the coverings
were torn down—

What was still there, waiting?

What was exposed, yearning to be held?

Write what hasn't left you,
Write what you've always known.

YOUR LETTER
BEGINS HERE

This is your letter. Not the
one written for eyes that cannot
see you. But the one that
recognizes you.

There are truths buried so
deep they only come out
when given paper and silence.

Begin where you still feel it.

Your Letter Begins Here

What was offered here
does not need a reply.

Some things
root deeper
when given
space.

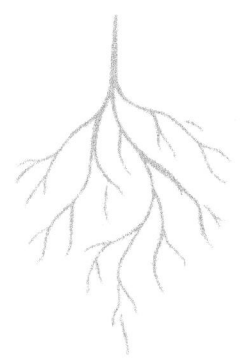

YOUR TURN TO SPEAK

What have you believed about yourself
that was never yours to carry?
If you were always enough, how would
your voice sound today?

You were not too much.
You were always enough.

The Season of Returning

You do not rise alone this time.

You Were Always the Soil

You were never what you lost.
You were what you held.
What you tended in silence.
What you carried before you ever bloomed.

They looked for blossoms.
They missed the way you held the roots
together when everything was falling apart.
You were not the weather.
You were the ground that absobed it.

You were the soil.
Even when it cracked.
Even when it dried out.
Even when no one stayed long enough to see
what lived below the surface -
you were still holding.

Still soft.
Still sacred.

And now, what was held in silence
is being called to light.

You were not forgotten.
You were not left behind.
The roots remembered even
when you forgot your way.

The soil kept its promise.

And now, so can you.

"The cracks weren't your ending. They were your opening."

What Grows Because of You

You don't need to bloom loudly to change
the landscape.
The things that grow because of you might
not speak your name.
They might rise slowly in someone else's season.
But they are real. They are sacred.

The way you stood, when no one saw.
The way you softened, even after the storm
The way you stayed rooted when
everything else pulled rway—
those choices made room for something holy.

You are not just healed.
You are healing.

Let it grow.

Where will you root from here?

Now that the silence has spoken
and the soil has held you...

What are you now willing
to carry in the light?

What in you is ready to be seen,
named, or shared–even gently?

THE
SECOND
ROOT

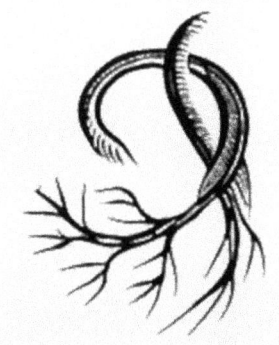

There were two roots beneath the surface.

The first, everyone spoke of.
It broke the soil.
It sprouted tall.
It caught the sun in its open leaves.

The second was quieter.
It didn't rise.
It reached sideways—into stone, into silence,
into places no one would ever see.

It was the second root that held the hill through the long storm.
It was the second root that kept the first from tipping
when the winds returned.

But no one thanked it.
No one painted it into the story.

It remembered anyway.

The second root didn't grow to be noticed.
It grew to hold.
It grew to protect.
It grew to become a

legacy of strength
no eye would trace.

Not all resilience rises.
Some of it deepens.

What holds you does
not always ask to
be seen.

Some things stay so
that something else
can begin.

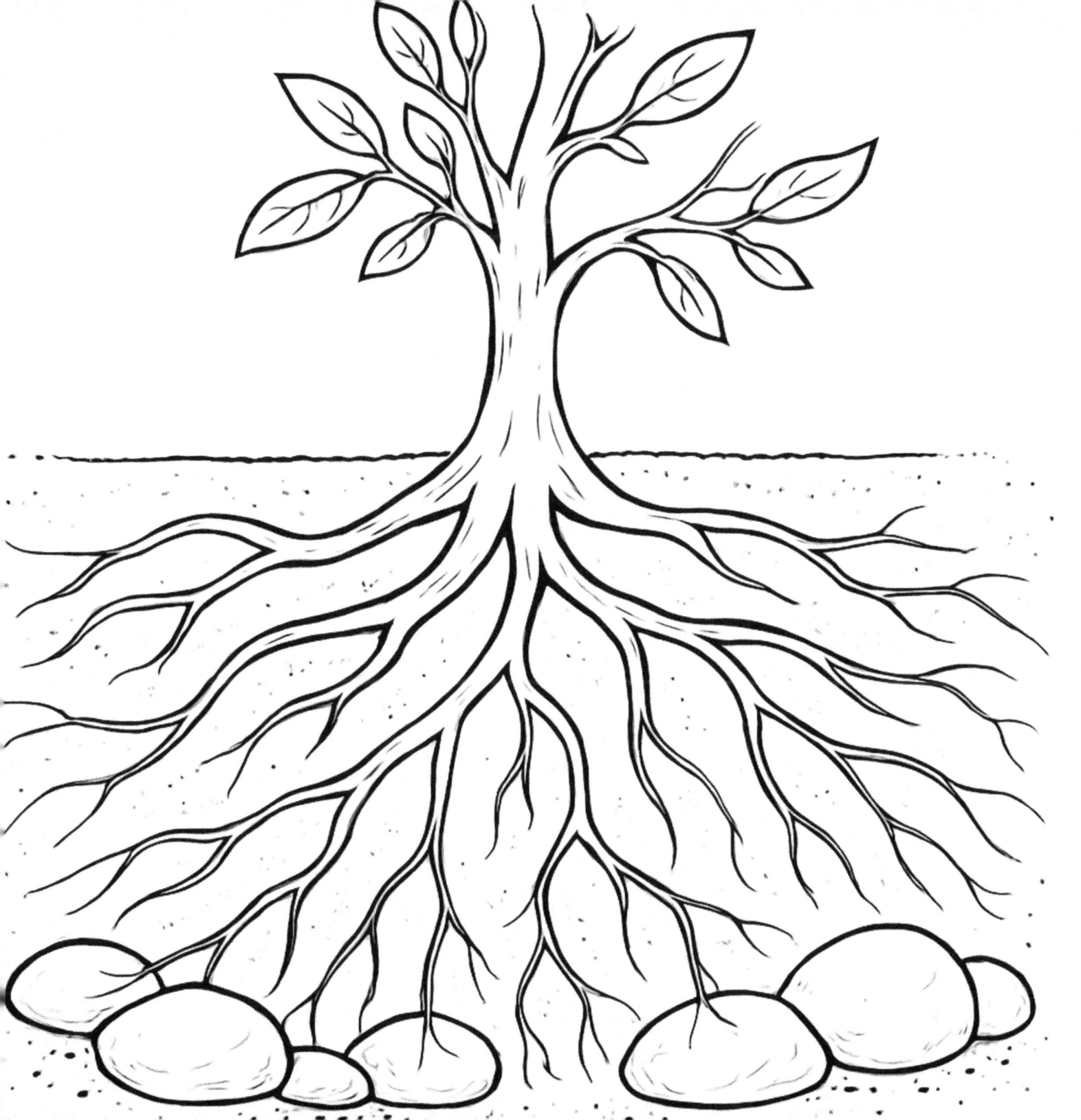

Some strength is
not seen because
it was never meant
to leave.

THE ROOTS WITHIN US

One root rose. One root held.
Both were needed. Both were true.

Inside you, the same choice is waiting:
To rise.
To hold.
To grow, unseen or seen,
and still be whole.

Before Anything Sprouts

Not everything that breaks the soil
was trying to grow.

Some things rise by accident.

Some things rise because
they're ready.

Some things stay still, and
that is still a beginning.

WHEN STILLNESS IS A BEGINNING

Name something in your life that hasn't moved – but might already be growing.

_____

_____

_____

_____

_____

Stillness
does not mean
nothing is happening.

"The seed doesn't speak, but it remembers.

Some things stay
so that
something else
can begin.

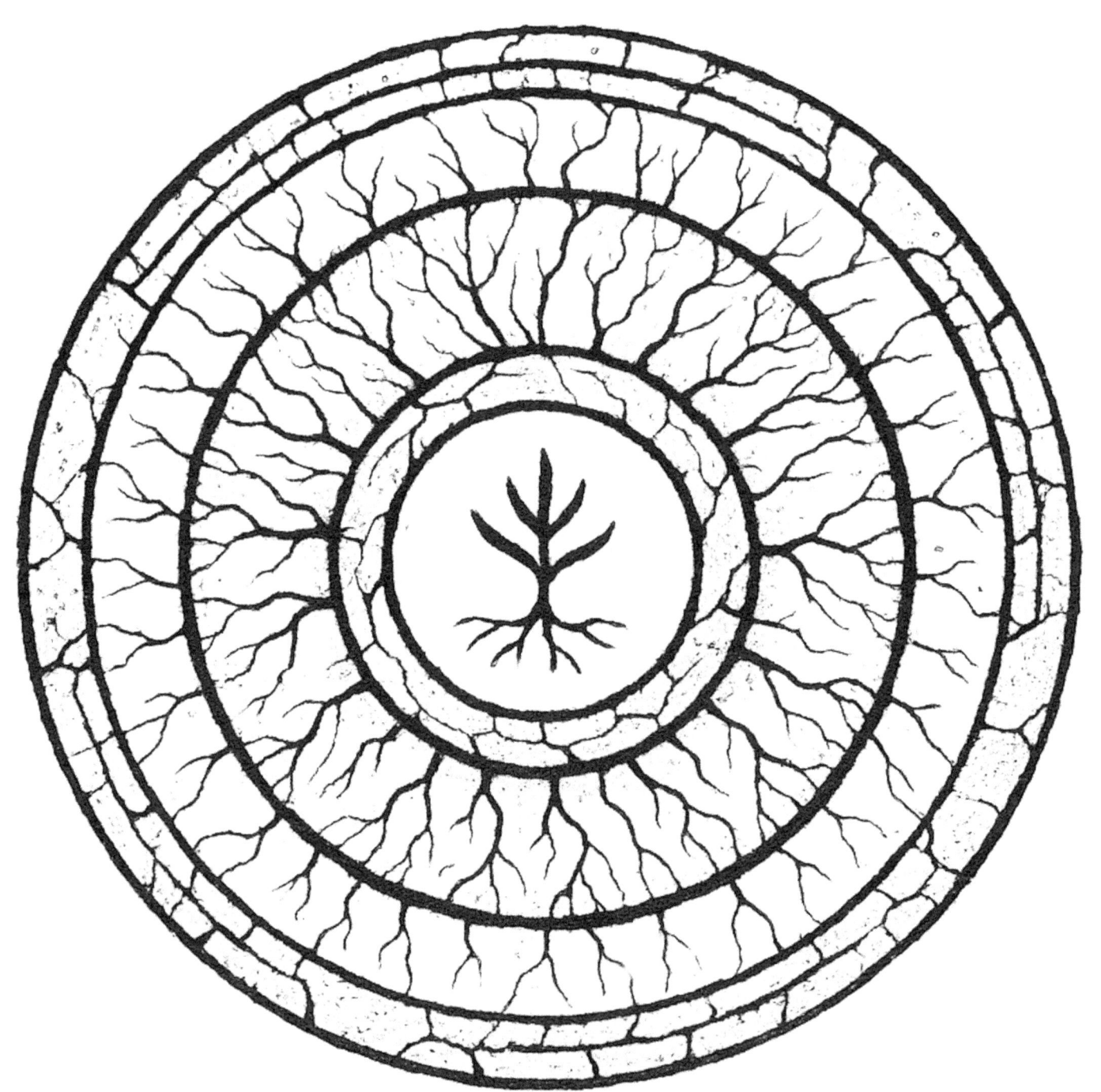

What Do You Remember Without Words?

There are things your body knows, your spirit carries, and your roots remember — even if you've never spoken them.

What truth have you carried in silence?

_____

_____

_____

_____

_____

The Root
That Stayed

There was once a tree that leaned over the mouth of a ravine.
Its trunk arched toward the sun, and its roots reached deep —
but not just into the soil.

Beneath that tree, hidden under years of storm and silence,
grew a second root.

No one ever saw it.
No one celebrated it.
But it was there.

It did not stretch upward.
It did not chase bloom.
It curled sideways — into rock, into dark, into the unseen.

When winds howled and the earth cracked with thirst,
it was not the outer roots that saved the tree.

It was the second one.

The one that worked its way through stone and silence.
The one that never asked to be named.
The one that only grew to hold.

And when the rains returned,
when the light found its way back,
the tree bloomed wide.

Everyone whispered of its beauty.
Of how it survived.
Of how it stood.

But it knew.

It knew what held it.
It knew what never let go.

And if you bent close to the ground,
if you pressed your palm into the dirt and waited,
you could still feel it—

the second root,
quiet and whole,
 still holding.
 For no one.
 But the tree.

The Thing That Never Moved

Name something in your life that never tried
to rise--but never left. What held, even when
you didn't know it was holding?

_____

_____

_____

_____

_____

_____

_____

TO THE ONE THAT WAS STILL THERE

You were not the loudest thing.
You were not the last to fall.
But somehow,
when I looked back—
it was always you
still standing
in the space I forgot to water.

I thought you were gone.
You had only gone quiet.

The
Tree That
Never Left

There was a village that forgot where the forest began.

Over the years, stones were laid. Paths carved. Walls raised.
And still, no one noticed the tree at the edge.

It didn't bloom like it used to.
It no longer called the birds.
But it was there.

It stood through the rebuilds.
Through the silences.
Through the seasons that came and left faster than names.

And though it held no leaves,
it held something older than branches —
memory.

One day, a child came asking questions.

Not about the walls. Not about the stones.
But about the tree.

"Why doesn't it leave?" they asked.

The village smiled. Or sighed. Or shrugged.
But the tree, still silent, answered nothing.

It didn't need to.

Because staying wasn't about being seen.
It was about remembering
what stood here
before anything else had a name.

"Some roots don't hold you back. They hold you upright."

The Things
That Grew
in Secret

There were cracks in the garden no one spoke of.
Tiny seams between stones. A quiet corner where the light rarely reached.
They weren't planted. They weren't planned.
But something began there anyway.

Not the kind of thing that wins ribbons.
Not the kind they name.
But something that grew because it needed to.

The gardener never watered that place.
But the earth did.
With old rain. With memory.

The roots didn't grow down — they grew inward.
Twisting around each other like they were hiding.

And they were.

It wasn't until the fence broke —
years later, during a storm no one remembers forecasting —
that someone finally saw it.

A small bloom, pale and quiet,
pushing its way through the stones.

It wasn't beautiful.
Not in the usual way.

But it held something that stopped the gardener mid-step.

Not color.
Not form.

But truth.

The kind of truth that only grows
when no one is watching.
The kind that roots where no hand has reached.
The kind that keeps blooming
even if no one names it.

The gardener didn't speak.
Didn't cut it.
Didn't move it.

Just knelt.

And for the first time,
watered the cracks.

What Grew in Secret?

What part of you began growing when no one was looking?

When you weren't ready, when no one asked,
when you felt alone —what still began?

What survived long enough to surprise you?

Let it speak here.

The Hollow
That Held

There was a hollow in the hill no one stepped into.
Not because it was forbidden,
but because it was forgotten.

Once, it might've been a den.
Or a root cave.
Or a wound in the earth made by water long gone.

No one really knew.

They just walked past it.
And it kept holding.

It held the cold.
It held the rain.
It held the sounds no one listened to.

And it never asked to be filled.

One day, a child found it.
Not by accident. Not quite.

They'd heard a sound — not a voice, not a word.
More like a memory echoing off stone.

They stepped inside.

It was colder than they thought.
But not unkind.

There were pieces of things:
a feather,
a cracked button,
a pinecone softened by time.

None of them meant anything.

And somehow, that made them sacred.

The child didn't speak.
They just sat.
And the hollow held them too.

They came back the next day.
And the one after.
And then again,
when the world outside didn't know what to do with them.

They never brought much.
Sometimes a drawing.
Once, a shell with a hole in it.
Once, just silence.

The hollow never asked for anything.
It only made room.

Years passed.

Others found it.
Not many.
Just enough.

They didn't speak of it.
But they knew where to go
when there was nowhere else to go.

Eventually, the child grew.
Moved on.
Became someone with keys,
and calendars,
and places to be.

But some part of them
was still curled inside that hollow.

Not trapped —
just remembered.

Because the hollow never needed to hold them forever.
It only needed to hold them
when no one else could.

And sometimes,
that's enough.

THE ROOM INSIDE YOU

There is a room inside you.
It has no door,
no need for a key.
It was not built by your hands.

It was hollowed into being.

Now there is a silence waiting
and an invitation
that cannot be mailed
or RSVPed.

And if you are still enough,
if you lean close to the wall of it,
in the quietest trace of breathe or time,
a softness might welcome you in.

This place was
not hidden.
You just weren't
ready to see it.

The Hollow Reveal

Everyone else saw the shallows.
I found the hollow.
I had to crouch to see it—a dark, sheltered
opening cut into the earth.
It was not empty.
Just out of reach, I could see the glint of
metal curl like thint of some unseen star.
Present mystery eludes even the most
watchful.
Step into the hidden spaces only when
you are no longer rushed. Crouch low and
widen your eyes until everything ordinary
falls from view.

Things I Carried Out

You didn't go into the hollow
to take anything.

But something came with you anyway.

A thought.

A silence.

A truth no one asked for.

The Room
That Waited

There was once a room you didn't mean to lock.
You didn't even hear the door close.

It happened slowly —
the way dust gathers
or light fades without being noticed.

It wasn't a room of secrets.
Just a room of stillness.
Too still for the pace you were in.

So you left it.

You left it for louder rooms.
For rooms with applause.
For rooms that mirrored back who you were trying to be.

Years passed.
Other doors opened.
Some slammed.
You stood in thresholds that never let you in.

And then one day —
you paused.
Not because the world quieted,
but because you did.

And something pulled —
not forward,
but inward.
Back to a place you didn't remember
until your feet turned there on their own.

The door wasn't locked.
It never was.

You just forgot how to reach for it without guilt in your hand.

You stepped inside.
The air had not changed.
But something in you had.

It did not ask you for answers.
It did not name your absence.

It just let you sit.
And feel.
And remember how to be held
by something
that didn't need to be fixed
to be beautiful.

This was not a new beginning.
This was a room
that waited
until you were ready
to come back
without needing to explain
why you left.

What Did the Room Remember Before You Did?

You didn't find the room.

It stayed—

holding your place

like you never left.

What did it remember about you

that you forgot?

_____

_____

_____

_____

_____

The Door Was Never Locked

It never asked where you went.
It didn't record the time.
It only kept the shape of you
etched in dust and stillness.

You thought it was silence.
But it was waiting.

A breath held for years.
A chair that never forgot your weight.

You came back different.
But it didn't flinch.

Because it knew
what you were before the forgetting.
And it loved that version too.

From the Rootkeepers

We didn't write this to fix you.
We wrote this to remember with you.

Because something sacred lives inside
silence and sometimes the only way to
hear it is to stop speking long enough
to feel the soil.

We listened. For years.

And what came was not a story-
but a stillness.

You're holding it now.

This isn't a book anymore.

It's a room.

And you just stepped inside.

You may not be ready for this page.

That's okay.

It will wait.

Some things don't end.

They wait.

What Was Left With You

The root you felt was never ...

Someone held
this before you

. . .

And now it's yours—
until it's not.

You are not the end
of this.

You are the echo.

Let it live
through you.

Then let it go.

you stayed
and the root
remembers

The One Who Stayed

Moses Peraza
did not come to teach.
He came to remember.
Not everything that
mattered was spoken.

He is the keeper of Still Light Press —
a house built not of answers,
but of echoes.

This is not his first book.
But it may be his most honest.

Moses Peraza

ABOUT THE AUTHOR

Moses Peraza writes the way roots grow-
quietly, steadily, beneath the surface.
His work doesn't rush. It returns.
With a voice shaped by grief and stillness,
Moses offers more than pages-he
offers presence
'Rooted' is his most honest work yet-part
of a growing body of words that honor
what blooms unseen.

To explore more of his work, visit
www.stilllightpress.com

ABOUT THE PUBLISHER

Still Light Press was founded by Moses Peraza
with a vision:
to bring light to the quiet corners of the soul.
Our mission is to offer stories, reflections,
and creative works that encourage healing,
inspire contemplation,
and support personal growth.
We believe in the transformative power of the
written word
and are honored to be part of your journey.

Moses Peraza

www.stilllightpress.com